ASSISTED LIVING

ASSISTED LIVING

Demi-Sonnets by Erin Murphy

BRICK ROAD
POETRY PRESS

Brick Road Poetry Press
www.brickroadpoetrypress.com

In memory of my mother-in-law, Ann Palmer De Prospo, 1914–2013

Library of Congress Control Number: 2018941355
ISBN: 978-0-9979559-4-1

Published by Brick Road Poetry Press
513 Broadway
Columbus, GA 31902-0751
www.brickroadpoetrypress.com

Brick Road logo by Dwight New

Table of Contents

I.

II.

III.

I.

Reverse Alchemy

Forget bullion bricks
and gaudy chains around
the neck. I'm perfecting
the long tradition of turning
gold to lead. See: autumn
leaves. See: lust. See: everyone
you've ever loved who's dead.

Trees Are Social Creatures

after Peter Wohlleben

They lean away from fellow trees
to share the sun and pump sugar
to stumps of long-gone friends.
Their roots interlock like fingers,
like my grandparents' hands clasped
across their nursing home room.
When one dies, the other dies, too.

Lessons from the Pygmy Mole Cricket

It leaps from the pond's surface,
tiny oars of spring-loaded legs
propelling it from a predator's grasp.
Water, it knows, is surprisingly
thick, viscous. We, by contrast, feel
mostly leaden, convinced the hard
earth that holds us is thin, vicious.

Paperclip

How you began as waxed ribbon
during the late Crusades. How your
curves are called *tongues* as if they
have something to say. How in nervous
conversation, I pry you into a silver
snake. How, unlike me, you've
learned to bend, not break.

Rockwell's Models Reunite

They were paid five bucks a pop:
the kids in PJs at Santa's knee,
the blond girl rescued from a flood,
the trumpet-playing carrot-top. The boy
from the barbershop keeps his hair
cropped to a buzz and like the others,
yearns for a time that never was.

Hand

The hole in your palm
is an open window, the sash
thrust high in its socket.
I press a coin-sized crumb
of hope in your hand and it
disappears. Then your hand
disappears in your pocket.

Teeth

Long-neglected picket fence,
ragged chits littering the stockroom
floor, a prized collection of brooches
carved from bones. Open wide
for the mirror. Smile. Find
your weathered name among
the crooked tombstones.

Pulse

The drum that thrums in
blood, a sump pump humming
in a flooded basement, Bedouin
plodding under the plunging sun.
Feel it in your thumb, from
sternum to scrotum. Da-dum,
da-dum, da-dum. Done.

Lung

A raft in a backyard pool,
strand of thread spooled and
unspooled, the sagging bag
in the chemo treatment room,
a cyclist chugging up and coasting
down a hill. We want to inhale
our days. We want our fill.

Hair

Women tweeze, shave, pluck, and wax.
Boys will it to sprout on chins and chests.
Men mourn each stray clinging to the sink.
How we find each other across a crowded
room. The first thing to go when we flush
our blood with poison, hoping we won't
have to leave the party too soon.

Faith 101

Always sit in the balcony
at the ballet so you can't
hear the grunts and thuds
of each dancer. To keep
your faith, keep your
distance: God, the almighty
rhetorical answer.

After the Worst Thing Happens

After the tears and bottomless grief
and hours spent staring at the night
ceiling with tight teeth, after the will
to move leaks from your body like ink
from a pen, there is a feeling of relief.
The worst thing that can happen
has happened and can't happen again.

Picture Yourself on Your Loneliest Day

Someone has died: your partner
or the last living relative who could
imitate your mother's laugh. You wear
the cloak of movie cinema darkness.
Instead of a table for one, you choose a stool
at the lunch counter where they let you
start a tab. Happiness is being less sad.

She Marries the Ocean

Seagulls are her bridesmaids.
The wind styles her hair. There's
no need for a dress. She wades
naked to her hips, her nipples,
her neck. The ocean speaks in
waves. Does it promise to take
this woman? *Yes, yes, yes.*

Inventory

On her desk, her husband finds my
name and a circled deadline. *I'm sorry*,
he emails, *but B. has just days to live.*
A sudden blood infection, sepsis.
In my mind: those scattered papers,
scrawled notes, the unfiltered image
of what she—we—will leave behind.

Empty

An empty belly is a baby's rattle,
a tin cowbell without a clapper.
She learned to make an apple last
for hours, hid packs of crackers
from her younger brother. Now
a mother with a full pantry, she can't
drown out the sounds, the hunger.

Jack at 3

It's like a storm swept away
a bridge in his brain. He'll never
walk, talk, play lacrosse, or catch
a lightning bug. When held,
his solid body clenches tight.
The doctors call it reflex.
His mother knows it's a hug.

Grieving Mother Behind the Scenes

She can't wear contacts. Each lens
is a tiny raft in a flood, clinging to her
spongy cheeks. She rummages
for the clunky frames from the strip
mall. Who is this smudged woman
in the mirror? Why on God's earth
are there caskets this small?

Hurricane's Wake

The waitress spends two hours
and 25 bucks to get to work
after the storm. A diner complains
that his burger is medium well,
not well done. If she's lucky,
she'll make just enough in tips
to get home.

Action

A man shoves a stranger
onto the subway tracks.
The train approaches like
a high-speed halo. Between
sinner and saint is a rail-thin
gap, a fissure. Bystanders jump
at the chance to take a picture.

Good Measure

A baby panda is as big
as a butter stick. A deck
of playing cards equals
one serving of meat.
A bullet's the size of
your pinky tip. We need
oceans to measure our grief.

Safety Drill

In the event of an active shooter,
run in zigzags behind the school,
my daughter is told. It's harder
to hit a moving target. Run across
the field to the woods. Don't cower.
But: so many moving targets,
so many wind-blown flowers.

Foul

A father fell from the upper deck
trying to catch a foul ball for his son.
Another fan shielded the boy so
he wouldn't have to see his dad die.
More than half a million civilians
have been killed in Iraq since 2003.
Which of these stories makes you cry?

The World Reduced to Fists

after Reginald Dwayne Betts

The world reduced to triggers,
to epithets that rhyme with trigger,
to words launched like surface-to-air
missiles. To rumbling stomachs
of hungry kids, to drinking water
the color of piss. The world reduced
to fists. The world reduced to this.

Exonerated

The innocent man is freed
after 19 years in jail. He's afraid
of the TV remote and steel
silverware. He's trained himself
to avoid looking anyone
in the eye. He knows he should
be angry. But oh, the sky.

II.

Childhood Under Glass

Summer night, full moon, bare feet
in dry grass, your children catching
fireflies. Soon they will rip apart
the undersides like you did once
upon a time. Their tiny fingertips
will glow with bioluminescent
light until each one dulls, dulls, dies.

Landline

The phone number of my childhood
home. Once I propped our rotary beast
on my lap and asked the operator to connect
me to my friend Beth. I said: *She has*
red hair and a white cat and she can die
from bee stings. 288-9041, 288-9041.
If you dial it now, it rings and rings.

Those Kids Who Played
in Storm Drains

Their skateboards loud as freight trains.
The boy in sixth grade who wore black
eyeliner. The day I followed him there,
ignoring my mother's warnings about
the toddler swept out to the bay. The curve
of concrete under designer jeans bought
on layaway. Echo of my words, my name.

Gift Shop Flowers

They're upright and proper like
Emily's mother who spent all summer
stabbing a needlepoint Christmas crèche.
You were sloppy in all the right ways:
late-night Scrabble games, pets on the bed.
I toss the vase of carnations in the trash
and bring you a fist full of baby's breath.

I Want to Remember My Mother

in those frayed cutoff fatigues,
her shaggy post-divorce hair
frosted at the tips, one bare foot
on the clutch, the other gunning
the gas, Janis on the radio
belting out a scratchy anthem
to everything that cannot last.

Worth

You can fall in love with a rich man
just as easily as you can fall in love
with a poor man, our 7th grade teacher
told the class. She spoke as if bequeathing
precious pearls. It took me thirty more
years in the world to learn that her advice
stung the boys as much as it did the girls.

Relatable

There is always a boy
writing about a fast car
and a song on the radio.
There is always a girl
writing about said boy
as she sits in her room
staring out the window.

Climate Change of Heart

In the photograph his eyes are blue.
Now they're the surface of a frozen
lake. He loved you then. He loved you.
Yesterday it was a balmy 50 degrees.
Today it's minus 2. There's no such
thing as climate change. Say it. Say it
till it's true.

Letter Found in a Drawer

The writer ignores margins
as if the page were a too-tight
dress stretched to the seams,
as if the world will provide
the dreams she itemizes
in each careful loop. Who is
this girl? She is—was—you.

Folktale

Once upon a time, a woman with blond
curls visited a village by the Bering Sea.
Such white hair, the children exclaimed,
likening it to ptarmigan wings. Such a big
qengaq, one boy giggled, tugging at her
sharp nose. *Such a small mind*, the woman
observed, thinking of her own.

When I Won a Poetry Prize

My daughter, then five, begged me
to buy *a warehouse full of pink light-up*
sneakers in every size so that she'd have
a lifetime supply. Instead, we got vinyl
siding. Her feet are now bigger than mine.
My mind flashes to an image of those
shoes blinking, blinking in the night.

What Comes Next

A boy begins to feel his own
rough stubble, rough stumble
into the world. He says *no*
and *no* and then *yes yes yes.*
He catches a whiff of October
and wishes he were mowing
a soccer ball across damp grass.

Living Across from the Junior High

During fire drills, students gather in front
of my house, coatless in winter, their voices
rising like bird chatter into empty tree
branches. Girls tease boys and boys mold
snowballs to toss at girls, thrilled by this
brief release from pent-up learning.
It's 20°, but they are burning, burning.

Fall, Central Pennsylvania

Twang of a basketball
on the street, teen dribbling
his way to a pickup game,
the sky a bruised backdrop
for barren trees, cracked
macadam court lacquered
with golden ginkgo tears.

Small Town

My neighbor returns from this week's chemo.
Her friend—a local judge—pedals up
on a 3-speed. She's here to administer
a foot massage. I don't want much. To live
in a town where people ride bikes with baskets,
a place where people show up, take your
beleaguered feet in their hands and rub.

Trick-or-Treat

Halloween night, two black bears
tramped through town. The next day,
we awoke to a blur of fur on the front
page of the local paper. Had we passed
them on the sidewalk, my son a werewolf
under the full moon? Yes, I'm certain
we waved and praised their costumes.

Things Are Cuter in Twos

One Yorkie pup? Sweet enough.
Two? *Adorbs!* The singleton toddler
you'd never notice is *awww*-worthy
with his twin. My beau with double
vision can't thread a needle or drive
at night. But he loves both of me.
What can I say? We're a delight.

Current Conditions

I don't want to hear the weather
from the chipper morning fellow
who recommends an umbrella
or a lightweight summer sweater.
It's every other earthly matter—
money, sex, my middle-aged bladder—
that needs a daily fortune teller.

In the Not-So-Subtle Dream

the wolf-twin of our dog moves in,
eats our meat, paces our halls.
From my reading chair, I reach
down to stroke the wrong beast.
It leaps up and bares its razor teeth,
sharp metaphor for the world
beyond these walls.

Dia de los Muertos

Here is a candle, Dad, and a handful
of marigolds. Here is my face
hollowed with charcoal, my paint-
stitched lips. I offer tobacco leaves,
Macintosh apples, a photograph
of your fourth ex-wife. Still you
sleep like you slept through life.

My Father's Story

I found a story you wrote
in those small block letters,
your attempt to control
the world one word at a time
like a wish. The setting was
an island, like you. Like you,
the story was left unfinished.

Generation Stuck

Cut yourself and you'll get lockjaw,
our mothers warned. *Scowl and your face*
will freeze like that. Every TV rerun
had a quicksand episode: Gilligan
or the kid from *Land of the Lost*
sinking up to his neck. Decades later:
screens, cubicles, debt, regret.

III.

Daughters of the Depression

Your mother and her cousins wave
from the luau, the pool, the edge
of hotel beds: Instamatic proof
of how far they've come, of the men
they didn't take, the meals they didn't
cook, the rooms they didn't clean,
the sweat they didn't break.

Prodigy

The last of too many children, she was
farmed out to a wealthy childless aunt.
For her third birthday: piano lessons
and a baby grand. Six hours a day in that
high-ceilinged apartment in the Bronx.
No excuses—and no bikes or skates,
nothing that might hurt a precious hand.

At Sixteen

She ran off to join Major Bowes'
All-Girl Band. First stop: Chicago where
she dropped her father's Italian name,
adopting the "Palmer" from the Hilton
downtown. She headlined with Sinatra,
Pat Boone. And now she shuffles across
the room, naked under a hospital gown.

Waiting

The woman who chop-chopped her hands
like cymbals now finds herself waiting
for everything: a sponge bath, a chirpy nurse
to wipe her *bum*, a son to blow in like weather.
Tick tick till lunch, though she can't stand
the food. Tick tick tick till dinner. Tick tick
tick. Here, even the sweet potatoes are bitter.

Heart Failure

She's a novel with too many plots,
a photo album with no room for another
shot, an overfilled balloon about to pop.
She's outlived everyone she's loved
or loathed, outlived the very word *cause*.
She is the last scene in a classic film
frozen on pause.

Dinner Companion

The woman in the dining hall
nods at everything. Would you
like some tea? Nod. How are you
today? Nod. She rearranges bits
of boiled chicken on her plastic platter
and speaks only when your mother
asks her name: *Oh, it doesn't matter.*

Activity Hour

The social director can't coax
your mother's neighbor to Bingo
or sing-along. She stares at the mint wall
in her room. When nurses come, she knits
her eyes tight. They scribble notes,
express concern. Her kids know better.
She's been like this all her life.

Cellulitis

Itis reminds her of *bite* and takes her
back to that farm mutt that tore her
10-year-old arm. Unlike teeth marks,
this is deep beneath the surface. The first
sign is her calf, glossy as the fenders
of the Impala she polished each Sunday,
shiny as her life's better half.

Osteoporosis

The pelvis of a twenty-something woman
is a plumb weight. A nonagenarian's
is as light as Styrofoam. The doctor
warns it could snap with a sneeze.
But your mother is a jet burning off
excess fuel. She wants to hear flute music
blowing through her bones with each breeze.

Oxygen

Even the word is congested
with consonants. She is
tethered to the humming mother
ship: 21 feet to the kitchen, 16 to
the bath. Wheeze gasp pant grasp
huff. She sucks it in by the lungful
and still it isn't enough.

Cure

Doctors have buried the word
cure. We now have treatment
plans and regimens and promises
of new vaccines. We have weeks
or months or years of progression-
free disease. We have years
or months or weeks.

Black & White

Pregnant belly under a fox fur coat,
Cape Cod home on a suburban street,
rag-top car in the drive. The new bike
beneath an aluminum Christmas tree,
a son's acceptance to an Ivy League.
This is her world in black & white.
Not pictured: the life she left behind.

Your Parents Fought Over Everything

What to eat, when to eat, what to watch on TV.
You wondered what kept them together,
this staid school teacher and showtune chanteuse.
Bicker, bicker, bicker. Cat or dog? New car?
New roof? Was it going to rain or snow? After
his death, she confided the sex was *sensational*,
which was more than you wanted to know.

Sad Things

Lottery tickets on the curb, unlucky
numbers rubbed off. Backyard pond kits
stocked with koi. Year-round Christmas
stores. Middle-aged bat boys. Go-cart
tracks overgrown with weeds and moss.
The garden wishing well your mother
always wished for and never got.

You Were an Only Child

The only one your dad taught to throw a ball,
ride a bike, shift gears in the blue VW Bug.
Your mother's companion at Broadway shows
and Sunday mass, the reason your folks sat
in the front row for every trombone solo
and line drive. You were an only child. Except
for the first three babies who didn't survive.

Tasks for the Living

You attach the walker basket
with the built-in cup holder, the one
that lets her carry a glass of water
to her favorite seat. Before you leave,
you test the battery in her hearing aid,
coax a curl with your finger dabbed
in spit, and kiss her papery cheek.

It's Easy to Mistake a Sparrow for a Finch

Both are small and plump and chatty
like little old ladies who squeeze
next to you on the bus. Sparrows
have an extra bone in their tongues.
Some elderly people do, too: a thin
cartilage of resentment that's perfect
for jabbing the young.

Your Father's Dementia

One night he woke your mother,
hovering over the bed. *You seem
like a very nice woman*, he said,
but my wife will be angry you're here.
She sat up on her satin sheet. *I am
your goddamn wife*, she told him,
and went back to sleep.

The Year Your Father Forgets Everything but You

He goes for a drive and winds up
in another state. A stranger takes him
to the E.R. *Did we have to come this far
to see a doctor?* he asks on the way home
where the wife he doesn't know waits
in her robe. You pat his hand and nod.
You navigate the night, the fog.

Lean-to

After a morning spent bathing,
buttoning, and hoisting your mother
like an overgrown infant, we find
the one sunlit table in an otherwise
dark sushi place and without speaking,
touch each of our fingertips together:
lean-to, temple, shelter.

Let It Be Known

That lake in New Hampshire,
its surface shimmering like
sequins on the gold dress
she wore on tour in 1934,
her body bobbing in pockets
of spring-fed cold. This is how.
This is how she wants to go.

Zephyr

You trapped your mother's black cat
in a cage and presented the armful
of squirming fur at her bedside,
vowing to brush him twice a day
and feed him tuna-flavored treats.
That was her cue. The hospice nurse
said our names. And then we knew.

It's As If

someone keeps finishing
your sentences without
knowing what you want
to say. The sky and walls
are grey. The floors: silt.
Did you do enough when there
was nothing left to do? Guilt.

The Problem with Death

The problem with death
is that there's no dry run,
no practice drive before
the test. You've got one shot
and one ball. No do-overs,
no drills. It's all or nothing,
then nothing at all.

It's Always 76 Degrees in Heaven

Think San Diego in summer
or winter. The air tastes like
water infused with an unexpected
fruit—pomegranate or persimmon,
water that tells a little story.
It's always mid-day in Heaven.
There's no darkness, no morning.

Acknowledgments

Thank you to the following journals that originally published these demi-sonnets, sometimes under different titles:

Summerset Review: "At Sixteen," "Waiting," "Heart Failure," "Osteoporosis," "Cure," "Black & White," "Daughters of the Depression," "You Were an Only Child," "Tasks for the Living," "Lean-to," "Let It Be Known," and "Zephyr"

Rise Up Review: "Safety Drill"

Barrelhouse (National Poetry Month feature): "Generation Stuck"

Review Americana: "Childhood Under Glass" and "Overturned"

Qarrtsiluni: "Trick-or-Treat"

Cheat River Review: "Reverse Alchemy"

Blackwater Poetry Month feature (Ireland): "Faith 101," "Letter Found in a Drawer," "Picture Yourself on Your Loneliest Day," "Jack at 3," and "Grieving Mother Behind the Scenes"

Section III was selected for the Seven Kitchens Press Keystone Chapbook Series and was published in a limited edition.

About the Author

Erin Murphy is the author of six previous books of poetry, most recently *Ancilla*, and is co-editor of two anthologies from SUNY Press: *Making Poems: Forty Poems with Commentary by the Poets* and *Creating Nonfiction: Twenty Essays and Interviews with the Writers*. Her poems have been published in such journals as *Women's Studies Quarterly*, *The Normal School*, *The Georgia Review*, *Field*, *Southern Humanities Review*, and *North American Review* and featured on Garrison Keillor's *The Writer's Almanac*. She is Professor of English and Creative Writing at Penn State University, Altoona College. Website: www.erin-murphy.com

Our Mission

BRICK ROAD

POETRY PRESS

The mission of Brick Road Poetry Press is to publish and promote poetry that entertains, amuses, edifies, and surprises a wide audience of appreciative readers. We are not qualified to judge who deserves to be published, so we concentrate on publishing what we enjoy. Our preference is for poetry geared toward dramatizing the human experience in language rich with sensory image and metaphor, recognizing that poetry can be, at one and the same time, both familiar as the perspiration of daily labor and as outrageous as a carnival sideshow.

Available from Brick Road Poetry Press

BRICK ROAD
POETRY PRESS
www.brickroadpoetrypress.com

Also Available from Brick Road Poetry Press

BRICK ROAD
POETRY PRESS
www.brickroadpoetrypress.com

Dancing on the Rim by Clela Reed

Possible Crocodiles by Barry Marks

Pain Diary by Joseph D. Reich

Otherness by M. Ayodele Heath

Drunken Robins by David Oates

Damnatio Memoriae by Michael Meyerhofer

Lotus Buffet by Rupert Fike

The Melancholy MBA by Richard Donnelly

Two-Star General by Grey Held

Chosen by Toni Thomas

Etch and Blur by Jamie Thomas

Water-Rites by Ann E. Michael

Bad Behavior by Michael Steffen

Tracing the Lines by Susanna Lang

About the Prize

BRICK ROAD
POETRY PRESS

The Brick Road Poetry Prize, established in 2010, is awarded annually for the best book-length poetry manuscript. Entries are accepted August 1st through November 1st. The winner receives $1000 and publication. For details on our preferences and the complete submission guidelines, please visit our website at www.brickroadpoetrypress.com.

Winners of the Brick Road Poetry Prize

2016
Assisted Living by Erin Murphy

2015
Lauren Bacall Shares a Limousine by Susan J. Erickson

2014
Battle Sleep by Shannon Tate Jonas

2013
Household Inventory by Connie Jordan Green

2012
The Alp at the End of My Street by Gary Leising

2011
Bad Behavior by Michael Steffen

2010
Damnatio Memoriae by Michael Meyerhofer

www.ingramcontent.com/pod-product-compliance
Lightning Source LLC
Chambersburg PA
CBHW032020090426
42741CB00006B/676